Charles G.D. Roberts

Northland Lyrics

Charles G.D. Roberts

Northland Lyrics

ISBN/EAN: 9783744789288

Printed in Europe, USA, Canada, Australia, Japan

Cover: Foto ©Thomas Meinert / pixelio.de

More available books at **www.hansebooks.com**

NORTHLAND LYRICS

BY WILLIAM CARMAN ROBERTS
THEODORE ROBERTS & ELIZABETH ROBERTS
MACDONALD SELECTED AND ARRANGED WITH
A PROLOGUE BY CHARLES G. D. ROBERTS
AND AN EPILOGUE BY BLISS CARMAN

SCIRE

QVOD · SCIENDVM

BOSTON
SMALL MAYNARD & COMPANY
MDCCCXCIX

To

Emma Wetmore Roberts

CONTENTS

Contents

Contents

A FOREWORD TO
NORTHLAND LYRICS

To E. R. MacD., W. C. R., T. R.

Sister and brothers, not by blood alone
Kinship inalienably dear we own,
Nor hearts close-knit in common joys and tears
And memories of sweet, familiar years
    That pledge the deep endurance of our love;

But also by the fellowship of song,—
One art, one aim, one impulse,— we belong
Each to the others! Therefore let this word,
Though poor, amid your Northland notes be heard
    For craft and kin and the loyal warmth thereof.
CHARLES G. D. ROBERTS.

NORTHLAND LYRICS

BEYOND THE GOLDEN GATES
OF SONG

Beyond the golden gates of Song
   Who treads with reverent feet shall find
The dreams and visions cherished long,
   The loftier longings unresigned;

The sacred memories that wake
   Our lives to noble yearnings still,
The quiet love no years can break
   Nor any earthly hour fulfil;

And many a dear and distant hour
   When gladness flooded land and sea,
And many a word whose tender power
   Yet stirs our souls to victory;

And so to win our lives' release
   From out the world's tumultuous throng,
We pass, with lips that sue for peace,
   Beyond the golden gates of Song.

A DEDICATION

These foolish rhymes of a foolish rhymer —
   One who has laughed and cried,

Northland Lyrics

And dreamed at times of a mood sublimer —
  I send, this Autumn-tide.

Not quite a thinker nor quite a poet,
  Though touched with the whims of each;
With much to learn and fain to know it,
  But never a thing to teach,

Except some rune of the gold leaves lying
  In the arms of the whispering frost,
While under the stars the geese are flying
  And the frozen winds are tossed;

Or the far, sweet word of the Spring-winds calling
  Our brothers out of the sod,
With the gold-bright drops of the Spring rain falling,
  And joy in the heart of God.

Poor scraps of dream from a heart world-weary,
  The rhymes you 'll find within;
But take at their hands the message, dearie,
  Of love from your kith and kin;

And say to yourself when you see them after,
  There is one who is foolish and fond,
Whose heart is moulded of tears and laughter
  And dust, and a dream beyond.

THE POET

God, give me breath for one brave fight —
For one great deed that the world will hear;
If not, then God give me night.

Night, with a candle to light the gloom,
And the comfort shadows and twilight cheer,
Crowding like friends in the room.

God, give me valor, and courage, and breath
For one great fight that the stars will see;
If not, then God give me death.

Death, with one candle to light the gloom
From the church to the door of Eternity —
Where, Lord, Thou wilt portion my doom.

Better the death, ere the beard be grown,
Than the idle waiting with sheathèd sword —
Uncheered, uncrowned, unknown.

God, give me breath for one fight more —
For one great fight in Thy name, O Lord;
If not, then close me the door.

. . . .

Thus sang the Dreamer, with hands along
The clanging strings — then, loosing his lyre,
He flushed with the pride of his song;

3

Northland Lyrics

For he was a poet, and lived in the gleam
Of the wonderful deeds that he touched to fire ;—
How brave he was in his dream !

KINSFOLK

Oh, fame may heap its measure,
   And hope its blossoms strew,
And proud ambition call us,
   And honour urge us through —
But kinsfolk, kinsfolk,
   My heart is all for you.

When stately halls are ringing
   With mirth and light and song,
Among the mazy dances
   The forms familiar throng,
And speak above the viols
   The voices loved so long.

When wandering far I visit
   Grey tower and haunted stream,
Beyond the storied casements
   Those earliest hearth-fires gleam,
And dear Canadian forests
   Grow dark around my dream.

Northland Lyrics

No strange and lovely countries
    Men venture far to view,
No power and gifts and glory
    Are worth one heart-beat true ;
Kinsfolk, kinsfolk,
    My heart is all for you !

THE NIGHT'S COMFORT

I.

I think the power of dream
Is the power the spirit knows
Over the crushing of fate,
Over the grinding snows ;
The strength of the Galahad-heart,
Stronger than barbèd spears —
The soaring of Chatterton
Beyond the beggarly years.

II.

I think the power of dream
Is subtle and fine like song —
Like essence of harvest fields
When harvest days are long ;
Gold and strong and rare,
Healing the dreamer's brain —
Filling his shadowed heart
With softened laughter again.

5

Northland Lyrics

III.

I think the realm of dream
Is true as the realm of day;
The houses our souls have built
Border the dreamland way;
The love that we may not reach,
The heart that is bitter cold,
Soften, when night comes down
With white stars manifold.

IV.

When the sunset fires are out
And the ashes blown abroad,
I throw aside day's rags
And follow my dreamland god.
He leads me into a place
Where dreams are woven me;
Valour and love and joy
Like a wonderful tapestry.

A SONG OF CLIMBING

Dim questionings of Fate and Time
  Beset our souls on every side;
Clouds thicken round the path we climb,
Yet strive we to the height sublime,
  Or perish if the worst betide.

Northland Lyrics

What worse could happen than to lie
   Here in the valley leisurely,
To watch the clouds go drifting by,
And feel our powers grow faint and die
   To one tame, weak monotony?

To see our mountain's shining gold
   Gleam far above us height on height,
And know the comrades loved of old
Yearn from it vainly to behold
   Our upward strife, our deeds of might?

Nay, — face the terrors of the way,
   The rock-pierced torrent's angry roar,
Grim walls that blind the eyes of day,
Sharp, swift descents for feet that stray,
   And awesome birds that swoop and soar.

Ah, better steadfast-eyed to scale
   The awful hillside hand in hand,
For never yet without avail
Did one true striving soul assail
   The barriers of the Mountain-land.

Rouse we our spirits to the race.
   Friends! Brothers! From the walls above
Leans many an unforgotten face

Northland Lyrics

Still wearing through its new-born grace
  The old sweet look of human love.

On! On! A hand for those who fall,
  For those who droop a song of cheer,
Ears quick to catch the Leader's call,
Stout hearts the gloom shall not appal,
  For lo! the towers of Home are near!

There watching by the open door
  Shine Cuthbert's heavenly eyes of blue,
There Muriel waits to meet once more
The earth-born loves she hungered for,
  To clasp our hands and lead us through.

There shall our lost ones wait, and there
  The height, the dream of our desire,
Supreme fulfilment, answered prayer
From lip to lip the watchword bear,
  The cry of Home! Through flood and fire!

IN AN OLD GARDEN

Sir Gold-Plush Beetle, in your crimson rose
  With you how goes
This life of perfume breeze and pollen gold
  Above the garden mold?

Northland Lyrics

Does any thread of longing in your heart
    At criss-cross start,
When some strange, wandering, bourneless thing
      goes by
    Beyond, against the sky ? —

A wide-winged moth, or twilight-weaving bat —
    But what of that ? —
Perhaps it set some wild, quick chord athrill
    Only the stars can still.

THE JOURNEY

When will I have to go ?
    Morning, or noon, or night ?
Will the lilies be white or the snow
    When I buckle the girths all tight ?

When will I have to leave
    This roomy old house and gay ?
Will my roistering fellows grieve
    When they hear me gallop away ?

Gallop away in the night
    From the light of the mirthful room
With their faces still in my sight
    As I set my face to the gloom.

Northland Lyrics

How long will the riding be
   Through the sunlight and fog and blur ?
Friends, whisper a prayer for me
   When I buckle on sword and spur.

For the road will be rough to the ford
   And the spirits will shout in the gloom
When I gallop and beat with my sword
   At the narrow door of my tomb.

ANOTHER COMPANY

Do you not know, my friends, that sometimes here
In this dim room with books along the wall
I entertain another company —
Where no wine gleams, no circled ashes fall ?

The merry jests we know — the narratives
Of brave adventure, which we tell to cheer,
When uttered by these other guests of mine
Ring, through their wide smiles, like a falling tear.

Last night they all came in, Ambition, Doubt,
Care with his heavy eyes and broken dream,
Life with his cynic smile and dainty hands,
And Memory, too, with her dear eyes agleam.

Ambition, golden-haired, was all agog ;
Doubt sat there moping at the window-pane,

Northland Lyrics

And Memory leaned against my dusty books
And counted her bright treasures o'er again.

I loved Ambition, for he promised me
Great things — green wreaths — a name to belt the
    world;
I glanced at Life who sat beside the hearth
And saw his cynic lips with laughter curled.

But as the night advanced Ambition left,
And Doubt and Life and Care, those brothers three.
So I sat on, until the dawn came in
Beneath the tears of wondrous Memory.

Do you not know, my comrades, true of heart,
That I pledge other eyes at other times?
That heavy-shouldered Doubt has his own chair
And brave Ambition fires my little rhymes?

THE QUIET PORT

There lies a quiet port across the sea
   Where the proud sail is furled,
Where the bright banner flares and flaunts no more
   That once waved round the world.

There the brave ships that steered for other shores,
   That fought the bitter blast

And dared the unknown straits, the frost-hung bays,
  Find harbourage at last.

And those white barques that sought the isles of
    dream,
  The lands of love's report,—
They too, though steering gladly otherwhere.
  Have found the quiet port.

There the dark night comes down around them,
    there
  The weary captains rest,
The homesick voyager bows down his head,
  The sage forgets his quest.

But yet, ah even while we fall on sleep,
  We are content to wait ;
Comrades, the land of our desire is near,
  This port is but its gate.

TO GOODRIDGE BLISS ROBERTS

All night the crickets sing among the flowers
  That watch beside you, sleeping on the hill,
And low winds whisper through the lonely hours
  That though we sleep our love is with you still.

Northland Lyrics

Some respite slumber brings us from our pain,
  For bygone days and hours of lost delight
Come back, and you are with us, dear, again —
  Though by your grave the low winds sing to-night.

THE CONQUEROR

Where are the eyes we loved,
  Tender and full of light ?
Where are the hands we held
  Stumbling on through the night ?
Gone — they are gone as a lamp
  Dies, blown out by a breath !
What have you done with our dear ones,
    Death ?

Where, from our eager eyes
  Withheld for a bitter space,
Do they wait till our hasting feet
  Have brought us face to face ?
Let us on to the Land
  That shines at the end of the quest,
Where they who passed from our side
    Rest.

Death, who took them away,
  Now they are yours no more ;
He who went through the vale

And drank of the cup before
Is Master even of thee,
  Yea, thou shalt fall at His word,
For He is over us all
    Lord.

On in the storm we strive,
  And thou dost lurk in the strife,
Ever subtle and strong
  In the very midst of life :
A touch and the face we love
  Loses the mystic spark ;
We are left in the lonely night
    Dark.

Yet we strive in the way,
  For out of the gloom a voice
Comes to us, clarion-sweet,
  Bidding our souls rejoice.
" I am the Resurrection," —
  Hear what the White Christ saith ;
He is thy Lord and Master,
    Death !

THE WINE

He breaks the seal, he pours the wine ;
We find the flavor somewhat hard,
But the color is divine.

14

Northland Lyrics

And we must drink it to the lees :
See yonder coward lift the cup
And drain it on his knees.

If we must down it, hard and sweet,
Bitter and mellow, we will up
And drink it on our feet;

Drink it like men of giant race —
Pledge to our host, who stands not far
With smiles across his face.

He knows the flavor and bouquet.
He forces it on every guest,
Grinning the same old way.

He keeps the flagon on the shelf
And gives us each a mighty glass,
But will not drink himself.

He will not drink, but we must drink;
So let us toss the stuff and bow —
Only the cowards shrink.

THE WINDOW OF DREAM

On the edge of the deep grey sea of sleep
    Between the veils of the rain
A casement gleams with the light of dreams,

Northland Lyrics

Glimmers, and fades again
While my heart goes keening out to it
　　Through the volleying gusts — in vain.

The window is set (O heart, forget)
　　In walls of looming stone,
And she is there, of the shadowy hair,
　　Waiting so long alone,
Whose eyes my soul would perish for —
　　O love, desired, unknown.

Now and again through the streaming pane
　　I see her longing face —
O love, I come, and my lips are dumb
　　And wan with many a trace
Of hungerings unsatisfied
　　For your eternal grace.

The long waves lift and the great winds drift
　　My heart to the sands of night,
Where the end of all is the looming wall
　　And never a door in sight,
While over the breaking sea there lies
　　The casement's lonely light.

.

A SONG OF HER SINGING

The wind at the casement enters, like a child's soul
  into the dusk,
With the cool, fresh scent of the garden, a fragrance
  of roses and musk.

Sing me a song, my love, and plead with the ivory
  keys
Till the soul of the organ wakes, astir with such visions as these,
While the golden day fades slowly among the garden
  trees
And I hear the robins coining their hearts upon the
  breeze.

Sing me a song, my love, of joys more sharp than
  pain,
The sweet, wild heart of dream athrill in the Autumn
  rain,
The pleasure that crowns us now, the joy that will
  find us again.

O love, with the beating and rapture of the spirit of
  life in your eyes,
Sing low of the passionate yearning, the heart's first
  faint surmise;

Northland Lyrics

Of the fairy quest, and the capture; the silence,
    rapt replies;
Sing softlier, love, sing lower, till the hush on
    spirit lies.

ANDANTE

Your fingers sweep the keys, and then
By river reach and iris fen
The long dead days come back again.

Smile on me once again, and so
Waft me on music soft and low
Down the far hills of long ago,

Where lonely sunsets blow and fade
For one whose haunted heart has strayed
At evening to the upland glade

Where he can hear the wild geese cry
Across the solitary sky,
And the cold sweeping winds go by

With broken words that laugh and weep
Like some one troubled in his sleep
By visions of the calling deep.

Strange forest-girdled lakes, whose moods
Lie hidden in far solitudes
Where no irreverent foot intrudes;

Northland Lyrics

Black, tossing rapids, through whose roar
A vague, great voice forevermore
Goes echoing from shore to shore;

All phases of that wilderness
Whose close communion used to bless
My boyhood in its loneliness;

All these across my spirit's ken
Sweep by on waves of sound, and then —
A sharp, sweet chord — they fade again.

The wandering ghosts have found their tomb;
And here, within this shadowed room,
Your gold hair glimmers through the gloom.

THE CHAMBER OF THE DREAM

I did not build a lordly house
Here in my heart, to stand through time.
I only filled a little room
With joyous scraps of rhyme,

And pictures that no brush could trace,
And music that no harp could make.
I hung the walls about with joy
And gold for my dream's sake.

Northland Lyrics

I pierced the walls with openings —
One for each season — windows four.
I wished to hold it through all time
So did not cut a door.

A workman from the goblin world
Carved me the ledges, fine and rare,
And bars of sunlight I had set
To hold my vision there.

With wonder of old tapestry
I hung the ceiling and the wall.
A clock, as every hour went past,
Rang a sweet madrigal

That some young poet wrote, years gone,
To some sweet lady, ages dead.
I had mock stars on either hand
And a gold sun overhead.

One window faced the April-time;
Grey poplars in a golden sheen;
Blue rivers breaking joyously
Like pictures on a screen.

One window faced the beautiful
Ripe Summer over all the land;

Northland Lyrics

The clouds that drifted in the blue
Were white as my dream's hand.

One window faced the Autumn hills
Where maples set the world aflame.
There the Red Hunter built his fire
And cried his lady's name.

One window faced a dreary place
Where spruce-trees crowded the low sun;
Where Winter set his spotless seal
On all that joy had done.

And thus, not in a lordly house,
I housed the dream I had of love —
I kept it there between four walls
With a mimic sky above.

And thus live I in my small room —
With tricks of rhyme and my sweet dream,
Watching the suns of all the year
Across the casement gleam.

Sometime I think the walls will part
And some one enter — then I 'll wake
To know the room and dream were made
For some real maiden's sake.

THE WATCHER

My heart is like an empty house,
The hostess being gone :
The halls are laughterless at noon,
The beds are cold at dawn.

My heart is like an empty house
That has not revel there,
With ashes on the hearth at night.
And winds upon the stair.

The glasses on the buffet stand
Unused for many a day,
The brazen fire-dogs grin and grin
A new, forsaken way.

The spiders weave along the wall
The sunbeams in a thread.
The echoes of old times drift by
Like shadows of the dead.

My heart is like an empty house
With all the windows down —
Save one, high in the cupola,
That looks beyond the town :

And ever at the window there
My soul looks out to see

Northland Lyrics

If Phillada, my heart's desire,
Is coming back to me.

When she comes back the fires will light —
The guests will all return —
The wine will fill the cups, all night
The scented candles burn.

The halls will glow with light of love —
The shadows slip away.
At noon our laughter will out ring
Across the golden day.

LOVE'S INCLUSIONS

When your lips to my hand you press
    Lowly, my dear one,
A moment out of the daytime stress
    Swift-snatched, my dear one,
I am a princess, and you my knight
Seeking a guerdon, armed for fight,—
(And the palace of Love looms near one!)

When we linger, while hours go by,
    Where woods are lonely,
With garnet leaves and a mist-blue sky
    Dream-deep and lonely,
I am a dryad that you have found

And fast to the life of mortals bound —
(Love's bonds are his young arms only!)

When your head on my shoulder lies
    Weary, my true heart,
I am your mother with watchful eyes,
    Dearie, my true heart;
With only a mother's passion then
For the boy so weary of strife with men,—
(For love has ever a new heart!)

When in your sheltering arms I rest
    Safely, at gloaming,
I am a child on its father's breast
    Hushed in the gloaming,
With all the rapture the child-hearts know,
Cradled and sung to, soft and low,—
(Love's heart is the hearth for homing!)

THE TOWER

Thy love for me is like a tower
    Whereto from strife and storm I flee;
High on the rock its steadfast walls
    Are set above the bitter sea.

Within its shelter safe and dear
    I hear, and smiling dread no more,

Northland Lyrics

The mockery of the ghostly wind,
  The time-waves breaking on the shore.

A PRAYER IN A GARDEN

Where this garden's walks are strewn
With the scarlet hopes of June —

Poppy-petals, rose-bloom tears —
Sun-dreams of a thousand years;

Let me lie till time is done,
Soft wrapt in dusk oblivion.

Let me lie, and dream, perchance,
Dim dreams of olden-time romance.

Let every golden lily blow
With some old tale of long ago —

Some lilt of swords, some song of love,
Some ballad to a lady's glove.

So let me sleep till time is done —
Till all the varied sands are run,

And Life forgets to turn the glass,
And drops his jester-bells, alas!

So let me dream, till these are done,
Soft wrapt in dusk oblivion.

TO LILITH

Behind such various vesture of strange dreams
Abides my soul, I know not its true form;
Nor have I faith it is the thing it seems —
Now hushed in calm, now crying of the storm.

Forevermore the dreams are as a veil
Of strangely-wrought enchantment to my ken,
Wherethrough my soul's eyes make my being quail,
Or bid me wanton with my joys again.

I have no knowledge of the thing it is,
Whether it be of fiend or angel born,
This much I know, belovèd, only this:
Beneath thy touch, of all its power shorn,

It yields glad captive to the joy that lies
Sweet on thy ruining lips and laughing eyes.

AT THE LAST

When all this trouble of life is past,
    This prating of honor and fame and sin,
The cry of my passion will find you at last,
    O love, and *our* life will begin.

Northland Lyrics

When God has broken His colored globes
  And crumbling ruin is wide and far,
Our love will flame through the wreck of things
  And build us a lovelier star.

The pigmy shadows which stand and leer
  And rob my soul of its strength to do;
The little duties which earth makes clear
  To hold me far from you;

The abnegations, the fears, the dooms,
  That immure your heart from my soul's great love;
These things will shrivel before God's eyes
  And fade in the fire thereof.

Then through the tumult of shattering dreams,
  The shriek and blur of the starry tides,
My love will lead you by quiet streams
  Where our wild joy abides.

Our lips will recapture the first dear kiss,
  And life's long fever which burned unquenched
Your eyes will blot from my heart forever —
  A brand in the white dews drenched.

Northland Lyrics

"WINTER WARMS HIS FREEZING HAND"

Winter warms his freezing hand,
Bends his head and leans low down,
Where the sunset fires the land
Just behind the hills and town.

Winter melts his freezing heart
What time the screaming geese take wing
And the willow-blossoms start
Up and down the creeks of Spring.

Once I warmed this heart of mine
By the light of her sweet eyes,
Firing my horizon line —
Firing all these Winter skies,

And in dreams I scent the Spring.
Dreaming still, she beckons me
And with wild birds we take wing
Down the creeks of mystery;

Down where willow-blossoms blow —
Dreaming thus, I kiss her cheek.
Waking, I can see the snow
Lying cold above the creek.

Northland Lyrics

A WHISPERED WORD

To-night a word, a whisper,
  Through long, long miles there thrills,
To you beside the river,
  From one among the hills.

Above the town's sad turmoil
  Your listening heart shall hear
The murmuring sound of alders,
  The whispered word of cheer!

SUNSET

The hearth-fire of the universe
  To-night burns kind and deep;
We warm ourselves before it
  In converse ere we sleep.

For Love, the mighty builder,
  Makes boundless space a home;
We nestle safe and fearless,
  With infinite skies for dome.

THE VOICES

" Lonely, lonely," over the hill
Wails the wind at its restless will;
Close to your shoulder my head I lean,

Northland Lyrics

No wind so sharp it can blow between :
(" Only the bitter wind of death; "—
Hear what the whisper saith.)

Swift, surely, the ominous night
Quenches the sunset's coloured light ;
In your eyes the star of love is lit,—
No darkest hour can banish it :
(" Only the cold, cold hour of death ;" —
Hear what the whisper saith.)

Nay, not the darkest night can part,
Or bitterest wind, true heart from heart ;
Hold me close that we hear no more
The taunting voices without the door :
(" Love shall be conqueror over death ! "
Hear what the whisper saith.)

EX UMBRIS

Dear heart, the storm cries at the door, the snow is
blown about the eaves,
The wind from some wreck-drifted shore around my
lattice window grieves,
And ghosts of happier hours go by across the dark
tempestuous sky.

Northland Lyrics

The spruce-trees crowding up the slope toward the
    lonely dwelling lean,
Forgetting all the songs of hope they crooned us when
    the fields were green;
The wailing voices of the blast mourn for the golden
    summers past.

The firelight dancing on the wall and lighting many
    a pictured face,
The wavering shadows quaint and tall, the carved
    chair by the chimney-place,
Have each some wistful word to say of one beloved
    and far away.

And yet how longing brings you near! Just now, I
    almost thought I heard
From out the bitter darkness, dear, your voice and
    that most tender word,
The sweet new name you murmured low, that
    Autumn — was it years ago?

A shadow on the threshold stands — O love, can
    this be fancy too? —
With pleading lips, and outstretched hands, and those
    sad eyes by time proved true! —
Now gladly, faithful heart, I come to these dear arms
    that take me home!

IN THE NIGHT-SEASON

The joy of my art
And the love of my heart
And the lost, lost garden of young delight,
I came to these
Through the shadow-trees
By the gate of dreams in the night.

The daytime was cold,
And the world had grown old,
And bitter and lonely the light of the sun,
And life was chill
With the dread of ill
And sorrow of works undone.

Came night, with its tears
For the severing years,
And its gift reluctant of weary sleep;
And then — your hand
In that clearer land,
And your word for my heart to keep!

THE LAST FURROW

Mellow the grapes are,
Purple as gloamings that free.
Yellow the corn in the husk,
And scarlet the haws in the tree.

Northland Lyrics

Wide winged the geese go,
Swift, and crying, and crossing the stars,
Foreseeing the snow.
The hoar-frost lies white on the bars.

This is the royal time —
The partridges out of their covers —
Each morning a rhyme,
And the sun and the hill are as lovers.

The cattle in stall —
The pastures forsaken and lone —
Firelight in the hall,
And the thistle-seeds withered and blown.

The last furrow turned,
With the great moon watching all white.
The oxen can rest now,
For the ponds will be frozen to-night.

"ON THE HILLS A GOD LIES DEAD"

On the hills a god lies dead —
Carl, the girdled one,
With the white stars for his bed,
For his shield — the sun.

Northland Lyrics

Brother to the crawling wind
And the sweeping snow;
With his hair adrift behind,
Forehead to the foe.

On the hills a god lies dead
With his sword in twain:
Down the East his grey soul fled
With the shifting rain.

Centuries it has been so
Yet I knew it not —
Still the hills mourn, and the snow —
He is not forgot.

Gnarled pines in the wind rejoice —
" Carl, the girdled one,
Gave to us his god-like voice;
To the sky, the sun."

On the hills a god lies dead.
Centuries have gone
Since his soul rose up and fled
From the crimson dawn.

Northland Lyrics

TO W. C. R.

The very thought of it moves me here —
The thought of April coming again
To our Mother St. John.   Excuse this pen ;
And the blot there looks like a tear.

How you will stand in the snow and note
The first faint odour of willows in bud —
The Indian-willow will flush with blood
And the robin will clear his throat.

The ice will swing at the brink, and flow
Seaward — a hundred miles let it travel.
The battered logs will hang on the gravel —
The islands will strain to go.

The geese will return to your hills — and the loon ;
You will find them all, some day, when you wake,
Trying the depths of a woodland lake
Or feeding in some lagoon.

A week will pass like a breath, and then
Up and along the creeks I know
The pussy-willows will scent and blow —
The catkins will thrill again.

Then you will slip from the bank and drift
In your slim canoe, and her gunwale's gleam

Will come to me in a happy dream ;
And your paddle will dip and lift

And speed her along, and through it all
The red-bud maples will burst and lean —
The swollen waters will snarl between —
Then I will awake, and call

And find that the valour of April and sun
On our Mother St. John and the Nashwaak there
Is not for me — so I 'll snuff the air
And dream how the thing is done.

SOCOBIE'S PASSING

Socobie, agèd and bent with pain,
At the time of the year when the red leaves fly
Crawled from his tent door down to the river.
" I will try my wrist and my skill again
And sweep a paddle before I die."

*Time falls — the wind falls — the grey geese draw on
There is silence and peace on our Mother St. John.*

Socobie, once a king of his tribe,
Once a lover, a poet, a man,
Launched his sun-scarred craft to the river.
" I will try my strength where the rapids jibe —
I will run her sheer, as a master can."

Northland Lyrics

At the time of the year when the pass is blue
And the spent leaf falls in the empty wood
Socobie put out on the merry river;
The brown blade lifted the white canoe —
The rapids shouted, the forests stood.

Down in the village the hearths were bright,
And the night frost gleamed in the after-grass,
And the farmers were homing up from the river,
When out of the star-mist, slender and white
A birch craft leapt and they watched it pass.

Time falls — the frost falls — the great stars draw on.
What voice cries, "Farewell" to our Mother St. John?

ESTRANGED

In my dreams I returned to my hills; for the life that
    I left,
The life of my waking, was drear as the pipe of the
    winds through a cleft
Of the mountains of old held sacred, but long of their
    godhead bereft.

When pitiful sleep drew near, and laid cool hands on
    my brow,
And kind dreams led me away, where my hills, like
    a great ship's prow,

37

Northland Lyrics

Stood forth to the northern wastes, my heart remembers how.

With the dreams I returned to my hills — and they
    were not the same!
Yet the winds went by as of old, and the red spruce
    murmured her name,
And down bleak alleys of pine the sunset quivered
    in flame.

Then I opened my heart and cried to the hills to know
A touch of their ancient kinship, their solace of long
    ago.
But the voice of the wind grew strange, and a hush
    fell over the snow.

AUTUMN DREAM

I overheard the Wind to-day
    Telling the Stream
The tragedy of Falling Leaf
    And Autumn Dream;

And when the Wind had finished it
    He laughed and fled,
With never any thought of all
    He left unsaid.

Northland Lyrics

And still the Stream went murmuring
    Of her own grief
Without a thought for Autumn Dream
    And Falling Leaf.

HAUNTED

It is a weird that cries across black water,
    And in my heart there is no rest at all,
But dim, unquiet dreams of ancient slaughter —
    Spring, Summer, Fall.

Sometimes only the wind on the frosty reaches
    With the low cry my heart has learned to know ; —
But in its voice that other voice beseeches
    Through wind and snow.

Sometimes night, with the hush and the starry glamour,
    Allures my feet to uplands far and lone ;
Over the dark horizon drifts a clamour
    Of words unknown.

And then I dream it is my own soul calling
    Through the blind urge of life's eternal deep,
Across the sobbing sound of spent dreams falling
    On death and sleep.

Northland Lyrics

THE WIND IN THE GARDEN

A wind is astir in my garden
Who spills the rose to death.
I will not, will not hearken
The bitter thing he saith.

A sinister, strange intruder,
He chills my heart with fear;
Wrecked dreams and ruined visions
At his approach draw near.

By the dial's menacing finger
The sweet hours wither and fall,
And the shadows leer and whisper
Along the garden wall;

For they know the viewless stranger,
With colder eyes than dawn,
The rustle of whose footstep
Tells me that youth is gone.

AN AUTUMN NIGHT

The night is like a mystic dream;
Slim alders bend above the stream
Wherein the last faint daylights gleam.

Northland Lyrics

The sere autumnal meadows rise
Smooth-sloping to the neutral skies;
Far off the lonely night-hawk cries.

The world is sad and dark the night,
And I who ever loved the might
Of Nature, whether dull or bright,

Am lonelier, sadder, than the chill
Slow stream that wanders at its will
Through these grave meadows bare and still.

THE WIND-CRY

O weary wind, be still, be still;
    Such bitter woe is in thy cry;
All the lost dreams of all the world
    On thy dark wings go by.

Thou voice of heart-ache, let me rest!
    Lo, thou hast gathered up the tears,
The sobs and manifold despairs,
    Of earth's unnumbered years.

Art thou the voice of Nature's pain —
    Or bearest thou, with dawning day,
The message of a lonely heart
    Too many leagues away?

BEYOND THE YEARS

The work to which his hands were set
  Went down with scorn and jeers;
His look grew deeper: " Even yet
  We 'll build — beyond the years."

The vision that his faith had wrought,
  Touched by the blight that sears,
Fell shattered.   But he said: " My thought
  Will live — beyond the years."

The dream that in his heart had rest
  Wrought bitterness and tears.
His eyes grew tender : " Now, the quest;
  Then joy — beyond the years."

He smiled to know his strength was gone.
  His eyes among the spheres
Saw strength and beauty at the dawn —
  In dreams — beyond the years.

Then the Great Silence covered him
  Too deep for dreams or tears.
Now the wind scatters at its whim
  His dust along the years.

Northland Lyrics

THE WANDERER

Across the lawn the leaves are shed,
The roses mouldered in their bed,
And where their frosty shadows spread
    The gaunt trees watch and sigh.

The moonlight, like a ghostly pall,
Casts its weird glamour over all,
Where the great house stands grim and tall
    Beneath the lonely sky.

Down the long path his hurried tread
Rings like a voice among the dead,
While by his side a stealthy dread
    Glides grinning like a gnome.

Her window, with a vacant stare,
Gazes across the garden square.
Only some marigolds are there
    To greet the wanderer home.

A SECRET SONG

O Snow-bird, Snow-bird!
Welcome thy note when maple boughs are bare,
    Thy merry twitter, thy emphatic call,
Like silver trumpets pierce the freezing air
    What time the crystal flakes begin to fall.

Northland Lyrics

We know thy secret! When the day grows dim,
  Far from the homes that thou hast cheered so
    long,
Thy chirping changes to a twilight hymn.
  O Snow-bird, Snow-bird, wherefore hide thy song?

    O Snow-bird, Snow-bird!
Is it a song of sorrow none may know,
  An aching memory? Nay, too glad the note.
Untouched by knowledge of our human woe,
  Clearly the crystal flutings fall and float.
We hear thy tender ecstasy, and cry:
  " Lend us thy gladness that can brave the chill;
Under the splendours of the Winter sky,
  O Snow-bird, Snow-bird, carol to us still!"

THANKSGIVING

  When beechen leaves are brown
    And barberries bright as coral,
  Let us forget the frown
    Of fate, and the longed-for laurel.

  Come where the maples burn
    In crimson and golden glory
  That Earth may hold in her urn
    The ashes of Summer's story.

Northland Lyrics

Faithless the birds depart
　　With musical chirp and twitter,
And Nature folds to her heart
　　Alike the sweet and bitter.

Then sing in Autumn's praise,
　　Nor shrink from the colder comer;
The joy of these shining days
　　Is deep as the bliss of Summer;

Winter in graves of snow
　　May bury, but hide them never,
For safe in our hearts shall glow
　　The light they have brought forever.

The woods, the hills, rejoice,
　　Each leaf a mute thanksgiving;
We sing with grateful voice
　　The pure delight of living.

THE FADING YEAR

Now fades the year, and in the sloping fields
The clustering thin ferns are misty red,
And in the wood red leaves are on the sod;

And down the paths among the dusky firs,
And down the shore beside the shining stream,
Come ghosts of other days and walk with us.

Northland Lyrics

Shrill pipes the wind, and all our world grows cold;
The darkness closes round us; on the hearth
The fires of home are kindled like a star.

Old voices call us, old ideals return;
The heart of childhood in us wakes and yearns;
Grant, Lord, it falter not again nor sleep!

HEIMWEH

The wind is just a far-off voice
    Beyond the pale-blue bound of sky;
Too weak to murmur or rejoice,
    I watch the moments drifting by.
So large the world; and ah, so chill
    The great pale sky, the shining snow;
The lonely wind is calling still,
    With a voice like human woe.

Now all my high ambitions fade;
    The things I hoped for seem so far;
From work once loved I shrink, afraid
    Lest some mistake that work should mar;
And all my longings turn to this:
    To hold my Mother's hand, to know
The rest of Home, the smile, the kiss,—
    And let the great world go!

Northland Lyrics

SURPRISE

Blind golden buds, we listened yesterday,
Somewhere where winds were cool and dews were
    tender,
To hear what older buttercups could say
Of skies blue-domed above the field's wide splen-
    dour.

To-day we bloomed, and thought from out the grass
To front the sun with half-closed yellow eyes,
But faced instead a white-draped toilet-glass,
And opened every petal in surprise.

GREETING

O glad brown earth, we greet thee,
    Freed from the shrouding snow!
Soon shall the shadowy forests wake
To starry bloom for thy dear sake,
    Soon where the rivulets flow
The crumpled ferns their sheaths shall break,
    The slender rushes grow.
O glad brown earth, to greet thee
    The skies of Spring lean low.

O sad brown earth, we greet thee!
    Hushed on thy mighty breast

Northland Lyrics

Thy graves lie bleak beneath the sun;
In vain the silver rivers run
   On their unending quest:
Strange grows this life, since death has won
   Lips that our lips have prest.
O sad brown earth, we greet thee
   For those who lie at rest!

SPIRIT OF SPRING

Spirit of Spring, draw near, draw near!
   Let the glad voices of the brooks
   Sing anthems out of shadowy nooks,
     And adder-tongues appear.

Bid all thy sleeping kinsfolk wake,
   The armies of the grass arise,
   White violets open fairy eyes,
     And crocus-flames outbreak.

Bring hope to souls that long have lain
   In blank despair beside a tomb;
   Let every resurrection-bloom
     Speak comfort unto pain.

In hearts where sordid cares hold sway
   And world-love dulls the sacred gleam,

Northland Lyrics

Re-wake the longing, and the dream
Of childhood's golden day.

Spirit of Spring, draw near, draw near,—
With leaf, and blossom, and the light
Unspeakable on plain and height,—
High-priestess of the year!

MARCH–WAKING

Before the dawn, when birds crouch close together,
A voiceless silvery stir the silence breaks;
So through the greyness of this mid-March weather,
Something wakes.

No green has sprung between the withered grasses,
No blossom stars the roadside's mossy miles,
Yet from the fields the frozen bareness passes,
Something smiles.

Not yet, not yet the time of song's full cheering;
Expectant silence all my heart enthralls;
Out of the woods and through the lonely clearing
Something calls.

BEYOND THE HILLS

The daffodils fling far the flag of Spring,
Their golden troop the garden-fortress fills,

Northland Lyrics

And bird-throat bugles greet the days that bring
  The daffodils.

Over the hills the Summer comes at last;
  But sad the light and sad the laughing rills,
And sad the golden flowers — since he has passed
  Beyond the hills.

FROM THE EARTH

From the earth our bodies came;
  From the sad brown whirling earth,
Knowing death, though not by name,
  From the hour of their birth.
From the earth our bodies came,
  And they shall return to earth.

To the earth they shall return,
  To a sod kept green with tears,—
Lips that sing and hearts that yearn,
  Stilled at last from doubts and fears.
To the earth they shall return,
  The brown earth kept sad with tears.

From the earth they shall arise
  Purified and strong and free,

Northland Lyrics

All of worth that here they prize
Made their own eternally ;
When from earth they shall arise
Purified and strong and free.

THE SHOOTING OF THE MOOSE

All day through woodland stillnesses
Of weighted fir and spruce
We 've followed on our springing shoes
The blood-trail of the moose,
And now the moon swings clear, and black
The shadows fall across our track.

All day above the crunching snow
Pierre and Dick and I,
With lust of blood, have sped along
To see the great moose die.
And now the night has come, and dim
The spectral drifts wreathe after him.

We shot him at the cabin door ;
The whisky-jacks cried shrill.
And when the smoke moved up I saw
The hemlocks waiting still —
The ancient spruces bending low
To his brave blood across the snow.

Northland Lyrics

Yea, brave his blood as yours or mine
And fit for better skill.
The devil's luck, Pierre! I know
The sights were fixed to kill.
To-night a bull-moose, plunging, dies
Beneath the comfortless, wide skies.

OLAF'S BOWMAN

Here is a rocky cave;
Where else could be fitter grave
    For Wolfgof, Olaf's bowman,
Flower and soul of the brave.

Asleep on the rocky floor
He can hark to the ocean's roar,
    And dream that the Vikings muster
Where the black tides tramp the shore.

Here in his Viking bed,
With his bow and spear at his head,
    He will hark to the voice of the wind
And forget, for a while, he is dead.

The waves will reel on the shore,
And the seaweeds will cover his door,
    And he'll lie with his head on his helmet
And his brave soul dreaming of war.

Northland Lyrics

When the brazen trumpet of doom
Shatters the gladness and gloom,
   Wolfgof, bowman of Olaf,
  Will rise like a prince from his tomb.

THE SHADOWY TIDE

Through the wide white streets of the little town
The bitter tide comes stealing down;
The night is astir with the wings of woe,
The shadows creep and cower low
At the creak of the frosts in the frozen snow —
And the aching tide drifts down.

The women and children will wake and sleep,
And the days will creep, and the days will creep,
And the silent tide flood full and deep,
And a shiver creep over hearth and kin,
And the gibbering shadows dance and grin
Till they fold us in, till they fold us in,
And we feel the chill of that shadowy tide
Which is cooling the world, and far and wide
Is surging up to the stars outside.

And in that day when the tide shall break
And the fulness of pain shall all pain slake
And the little city its rest shall take
From the long toil of life,

Northland Lyrics

The strong man out of his sleep will wake,
From dreams of child and wife,
To find his hair and his beard washed grey
With the bitter spume of the frozen spray,
And the dust at his lips that he may not pray.

I feel it cold at my heart to-night;
It creaks the stair and dims the light,—
A frozen breath before my sight.

TO AN OLD SHIP'S FIGURE-HEAD

You tasted the brine through the Viking years,
And gazed wide-eyed on the lifting flood,
With the measureless song of the sea in your ears—
Her pulse in your blood.

And now from the corner of this old room
You gaze wide-eyed at the curtain'd wall,
Where the wood-lice tick all day in the gloom,
And the shadows crawl.

Behind that forehead, all brown and scarred,
Do dreams of the wind-mad sea still move?
Dream on, for the harbor mouth still is barred
'Twixt you and your love!

Northland Lyrics

INSCRUTABLE

Her gold hair, fallen about her face,
Made light within that shadowy place,
  But on her garments lay the dust
Of many a vanished race.

Her deep eyes, gazing straight ahead,
Saw years and days and hours long dead,
  While strange gems glimmered at her feet,
Yellow, and green, and red.

And ever from the shadows came
Voices to pierce her heart like flame.
  The great bats fanned her with their wings,
The voices called her name.

But yet her look turned not aside
From the black deep where dreams abide,
  Where worlds and pageantries lay dead
Beneath that viewless tide.

Her elbow on her knee was set,
Her strong hand propt her chin, and yet
  No man might name that look she wore,
Nor any man forget.

Northland Lyrics

HAROLD

Up from the trodden sands lift his red plume;
    Shoot his maimed stallion, and sheathe his red
      sword;
Bury him there where the cliffs make a gloom
    And the cedars hang desolate over the ford.

Helmet and cuirass and scabbard of steel,
    Gauntlets and top-boots and clatter of spur,—
Dumb now the clashing from thigh-bone to heel,
    And harmless as dragon-fly mocking them there.

Such a great fight there will never be more;
    Harold alone there, with pistols and sword,
Shooting them down where they rode to the shore,
    Cutting them down where they rode from the ford;

Twenty long minutes he held it, and then,
    Shouting, came down from the pass overhead;
He turned in his saddle to cheer on his men,
    And the grey rocks that saw it were spattered with
      red.

Bury him there where the waters swing by,
    And the gloom of the mountain hangs over the ford;
With his feet to the rock and his face to the sky,
    And the grip of his hand on the hilt of his sword.

Northland Lyrics

Bury him there where the winds in the pass
  Will cry him the dirges the sere cedars know.
No tear will awake him of comrade or lass,
  Where we leave him to dream in the grass and the
    snow.

Only the flare of his singing red plume
  Like the flag of a hero will challenge the ford,
Till the last great " To horse ! " will blare over his
    tomb,
  And he 'll lead us again with his hand on his sword.

GREY GARRY

Grey Garry stood in the dusky stall —
Grey Garry, dapple-grey Garry.
He heard the birds, and the wind's footfall;
He heard the sparrows flutter and call,
Where the soft lights flush and tarry.
He raised his head from the scented hay —
  He drew his lips from the yellow grain,
For down the cool of the ending day
  He heard *his* laughter again.

Nay, Grey Garry, 't was but a dream —
  The wind gone daft or the trees unstrung.
Nay, dear horse, it was but a trick
  Of the Summer-wind, who is ever young.

Northland Lyrics

The writer sat in his lamp-lit room —
Weary and sad the writer.
He heard the wind in the outer gloom —
It held a tang of the woodland bloom,
As it did when the world was brighter.
He lifted his eyes from the scribbled proofs;
    He dropped the pen from his weary hand,
For somewhere he heard the clatter of hoofs —
    Galloping hoofs through a Summer land.

Nay, good writer, 't was but a dream —
    The wind gone daft or thy nerves unstrung.
Nay, dear boy, it was but a trick
    Of the Summer-wind, who is ever young.

SMOKE-WREATHS

These fading smoke-wreaths hold them all —
    The dawns and dreams gone by,
The lights and shadows on the wall,
    The gleams of open sky,

And all the vague, elusive things
    That haunt the halls of life
With sense of vast o'ershadowing wings
    And rumourings of strife.

How this small bowl of ruddy fire
    Can people all the room
58

Northland Lyrics

With strangers from the realm Desire,
    Beyond the gulfs of Doom,

Till all about me in the dusk
    The silence is astir
With gleam of steel and breath of musk
    And frankincense and myrrh,

While dream, adown the shifting breath
    Of myth and love and war,
Lures from the hollow vault of death
    Wild hearts that beat no more;

And Roland's bugle, through the night
    Sends forth its far weird fall
Where weltering and dense the fight
    Goes over Roncevalles.

Joan of Arc, and Héloise,
    Swan Helen, fatal star,
And Dante's deep-eyed Beatrice
    Go through the dusk afar;

King Arthur of the weary quest,
    Excalibur in hand,
Flashes, where 'er is sorest prest
    His lion-hearted band;

Northland Lyrics

The joy of battle fierce and strong
    Drifts through the deathly bars
While clash and swing of sword and song
    Clang up among the stars,

And strange wild sagas of the North
    Pulse fire through all my veins
As where across the sky go forth
    The Weird Light's shaken skeins;

Then slowly, as my pipe burns low
    Enchantments pale and fade,
Till, in the ash of long ago
    The last dear ghost is laid.

THE DEEPS

In mind's subconscious waters black and vast
On which thought's lifting laboured spans are cast
What blind germs wait the mystic touch at last.

There, teeming, blind, below the coasts of dream,
The pregnant voiceless currents drift and stream,
With doom and dread and rapture in their gleam.

With here,—to bloom when I shall touch your hand,—
Through bourneless darkness drifting for no strand,
A scarlet magic seed from some far land.

Northland Lyrics

And here, survivors from old worlds undone,
Strange thought-germs latent till a fiercer sun
Shall thrill them with eternity begun.

Valours and visions, impulse, dream, and strife,
Old ethnic currents through the core of life,—
With these the gravid sunless deeps are rife.

BEFORE THE GATE

A snow-swirl from the bitter blast of life,
A wavering flame before the winds of death,
A soul beat upward toward the feet of God.

With blind desire he battered against space,
And with the heartache of a child come home
He shook with anguish at the frozen door.

Sealed with the freezings of oblivion
The looming shadowy gates of God's abode
In awful silence stirred not to his cry.

And then a voice woke very far away
Saying, " You may not win to that pure light
Wherein the fulness of all joy abides

" Till you have won its shadow upon earth,
That white and strangest of all mysteries,
The perfect wonder of a woman's love."

61

Northland Lyrics

The grey and aching vision of the gate
Wavered before him. With unuttered cry
He shivered outward where the darkness leered.

THE LOUP-GAROU

The song I heard at the river's bend,
  Mellowed across the foaming " rip,"
That night in June when my pulses stirred
  To the dream my heart let slip,—
This is all I remember now
When the bees come back to the linden bough.

The song I heard and the face I saw
  While through the dusk I loping sped
Like some grey wraith the winds might draw
  Across the sunset's red ;—
This is all I remember now
When June has sweetened the linden bough.

I heard her scream as I passed the door,—
  The low log doorway where she stood ;—
It blended and passed with the rapid's roar
  As I plunged through the hollow wood ;
And my heart grows wild with the memory now
When the bees are back on the linden bough.

Northland Lyrics

Fierce gods who made me half man, half brute,
  Why add this bitter last touch to my pain?
Am I less than the reddening willow-shoot
  You soothe in the white spring-rain?
Yet me you torture to madness now
With the bloom and the bees on the linden bough.

KATHALEENA

Kathaleena! Kathaleena!
Through the green, bird-haunted valley,
  Through the brook-bright, windy meadow,
  Through the dim mysterious forest,
    All the birds are calling thee;
All the brooks their voices rally,
  Shout thy name through sun and shadow,
    Cry, " Bring back the light thou borest
    From our fields, Astore Machree"!
Kathaleena! Kathaleena!

Kathaleena! Kathaleena!
In the land where now thou strayest
  Have the sombre hills grown brighter,
  Have the birds a richer singing,
    Since thy lovely soul is there?
Surely, surely skies the greyest,
  Hearts the saddest, must grow lighter,

Northland Lyrics

Where thy tender voice is, bringing
Blessèd dreams and visions fair.
Kathaleena! Kathaleena!

Kathaleena! Kathaleena!
Ah return to those who call thee,
  Come once more to us who wander
    Through the ways thou leavest lonely,
    Vales that wait for love and thee:
Let no stranger-lands enthrall thee,
  Dream no foreign hearts are fonder
    Than the heart that longs for only
      Thy low voice. Ah come, Machree!
Kathaleena! Kathaleena!

ROSEMARIE

Rosemarie plays in the firelight's blaze,
  Her shadow is dark on the wall,
Her eyes are dim with a dream of him;
  (Ah how the storm-winds call.)

He will come to-night in the storm's despite,—
  (Dark is the woodland way),—
She hears the beat of his horses' feet,
  In her heart there is holiday.

Northland Lyrics

More rich, more clear, as the hour draws near,
    The clangorous keys rejoice;
In her jubilant heart such thoughts upstart,
    And music finds them a voice.

Of those eyes she dreams where the love-light gleams
    Warm as the heart of June,
On her lips the while the slow sweet smile
    Grows glad with the golden tune.

What the white storm hides in its drifting tides
    Will the eyes of dawn betray?
The cold wind calls from the mountain walls,
    Dark is the woodland way.

Ah sweet, dream on till the night is gone
    And the tender hope is dead;
In those dearest eyes the death-chill lies,
    There is snow on that shining head.

HIS WHIM

Because his dream was fair,
    His life not so,
He turned from his despair,
    To go.

Because his light was dim,
    The night so wide,

Northland Lyrics

He yielded to his whim
And died.

But when his heart had rest
Beneath the sod
There came to him this test
From God:

The one he loved in vain
To where he slept
Came through the Autumn rain,
And wept.

Then all his fancied peace
Returned to strife;
He groaned for his release
To life.

AFTER

Though Death has claimed my dust
For the earth's need,
Lent me a while on trust
By flower and seed;

Though Failure clutched me in
His iron hand
With that old look and grin
I understand;

Northland Lyrics

They neither can annul
    Nor make accurst
The light that through my skull
    Sifts still, as first

It did, when in my eyes
    (Which now are none)
It woke some dear surmise
    Of joy begun,

And those black frosts that stir
    In the deep wood
Told me without demur
    That life was good.

TO THE LORD OF THE YEARS

This rolling sea of stars
    Is dust before Thy breath
Whose pleasure makes or mars
    The halls of life and death.

Thy least desire is heard
    Beyond the vasts of space,
And being's core is stirred
    At turning of Thy face.

Northland Lyrics

The cycles of earth's years
  Are phases in Thy dream
Unblurred by drift of tears,
  Untouched of shade and gleam.

Yet of Thy will we are,
  And children of Thy word
With every sun and star,
  With every flower and bird.

Then grant we may not fail
  From out Thy vision vast
When life's strong warders quail
  Before death's icy blast :

But may we still aspire
  To things unknown, unguessed,
More near the heart's desire
  Than this poor body's quest.

TOASTS

Gentlemen ! comrades and friends,
We 'll forget our short purses, long woes —
We 'll all fill with port to the brim,
For I have some toasts to propose.

The ladies — old sweethearts and new —
The girls whom we once loved, and now :

Northland Lyrics

Marie of the glowing gold hair
And Lalage of the white brow;

Celeste, who was married last week,
Blithe Nell, whom I'd marry to-day
If she would write "Yes" to my prayer
And the papers would give me more pay;

The shopping-mad girls of New York —
The ladies of old Acadie —
The girls who are dearest to you
And the girl who is dearest to me.

Next! The ladies whose love is true love —
Not a bubble, to break at a whim —
Our Mothers! God bless them! and here's
Their health, to the stem from the brim.

Next! The pens that we shake at the world
And butter our bread with — buy wine —
Your pen, and your pen, and your pen,
And your pen, and Will's pen, and mine.

They have stuck to us through '97,
And brought no more joy than gold-plate:
If we work for the things that we dream of
They will stick to us through '98.

And last ! with a clinking of glasses
Here 's each to the hearts of the others,
And we swear, by the pen and the ink-pot,
To scribble, stay poor, and be brothers.

BEFORE THE DUEL

[*London. 1750.*]

To-night I am alone in my own chair
  Before the fire that good Janette has lit —
To-morrow, ere the sun is in the east,
  I, who love life, will be all done with it.

And so the thoughts that I have long held down,
  Of homely Devon and the mother-face,
Come surging back across my stricken soul,
  And all these years of ink and town erase.

I know how tears will fill the mother-eyes,
  How agony will chill her heart's soft beat,
When John takes up the news in Monday's mail
  Of death, behind Paul Rober's, in Grub Street.

O God, is this reward for all her love ?
  That I should cause her grief, because a girl
Who has no heart, nor soul, nor any good,
  Has set me at Lord Clare with her lip's curl ?

Northland Lyrics

I, who love life, and have my work to do,
    And joy to take, and little gift of rhyme,
Will leave it all for honour, at one thrust,
    Before St. Paul's can see the dear sun climb.

O honour, let me curse the shape you take —
    And love! I see a lady smile next week;
What matters it to her if he is dead
    Who but this morning kissed her glowing cheek?

So here am I in my familiar chair,
    And, else Clare slip, I sit for my last time.
Good-night, thou dear, far Devon — mother-face —
    Good-night, poor laughter, finery, and rhyme.

THE NOVICE

O soul above my soul,
    Who art myself and more —
The dream God gives to guide
    From door to door,—

By thy averted brow
    And wistful, grieved disdain
Teach thou this crying heart
    To conquer pain.

When hungry passions wake
    Wild tears within my breast

Northland Lyrics

The lifting of thine eyes
   Stills them to rest.

My eager hands would grasp
   Desires fond and vain;
On the far hills a voice
   Wakes to restrain.

O thou unnamed, austere,
   Make strong thy tyranny,
That I may·never more
   Long to be free;

Else let my spirit go,
   Unconscious of a choice,
Blown on by shifting winds,
   Deaf to thy voice,

Until my life goes by
   In joys more sharp than pain,
A core of wild sweet fire
   And April rain.

AT THE HEART'S CRY

Till the black-crimson petals of that night
Drew down to the gold vortex of strange dreams
My soul and body, wearied of the fight

Northland Lyrics

Of far ideals and clashing fierce desires,
I was as one struck blind by life's sweet light
And deafened by a myriad singing fires.

So was I glad when night's deep velvet rose
Closed over me and hid me from myself;
As on my northern hills the first soft snows
From grey skies brooding like an angel's wing,
Compassionate, where the last lorn maple glows,
Blot out all sad remembrances of Spring.

Æons it seemed the changing dreams went by
Sphinx-like, or smiling-eyed, or dim with tears,
While ages died along sleep's shaken sky
Where flashing lights of far-off battles streamed
And wind-swept clamors beat their way on high
Then fell on silence — and I knew I dreamed.

And then, across black solemn pools of fate,
Was it some cry of your wild heart to mine
That fading left the whole world desolate
And me sob-shaken with a vain desire,
As one who beats against a granite gate
On marshlands lonely in the sunset's fire?

ALIEN

Whom the great goddess once has kissed
    Between the brows
His heart shall find no dwelling-place
    Wherein to house.

The ragged mists shall be his roof
    Where mountains loom,
And swirling winds about his face
    With words of doom ;

The valleys when he walks therein
    Are kind and warm,
Yet ever drift across his soul
    Strange gusts of storm.

If weary, he shall stop beside
    An opened door,
Dreaming, " This hearthstone is my goal, —
    To wend no more."

A tumult as of snows adrift
    Shall fill his ears,
His heart-strings feel the old-time lure
    Adown the years,

Northland Lyrics

And he shall turn from that warm light
    With still regret
That dreams were made not to endure,—
    Nor to forget.

AT TWILIGHT

Out of the dusk, wind-blown and thin,
The shadowy woodboats gather in,
And twilight hushes the harbor's din,—
    Sleep, little head, on my shoulder.

The gold lights wake through the evening grey
In the little village beside the bay,
And a few cold stars gleam far away,—
    Sleep, little head, on my shoulder.

The sailor turns his face once more
Where his sweetheart waits at the opened door.
The lone light washes the wave-swept shore,—
    Sleep, little head, on my shoulder.

Here where the dancing shadows swarm
Our driftwood fire is bright and warm;
Beyond our window wakes the storm.
    Then sleep, little head, on my shoulder.

75

SLUMBER-SONG

Hushed, hushed the night comes,
   Day's cares are ended,
Put by your heavy thoughts,
   Rest, dusk-befriended;
Softly my voice shall weave
   White webs of sleep,
Soothing you, folding you,
   Peaceful and deep;
Doubt shall fade, pain shall flee
   Discord, and fear,—
Just your love murmuring
   Low at your ear;
Respite and comforting
   Soul-deep, profound,
Come while I build your sweet
   Palace of sound;
Gold through your drowsy brain
   Star-visions gleam,
While my song makes for you
   Dim walls of dream;
Hushed, hushed the night comes,
   Heart-pangs are ended,
Peace shall encompass you,
   Slumber-befriended;

Northland Lyrics

Fear not, for love is near
    Ne'er to depart,
O thou long-tried and true,
    Heart of my heart!

BERCEUSE

All pain, all sorrow, seem to fall
    Behind us infinitely far,
What time the sleepy robins call
    At Twilight's dusky bar.

Lay down your head upon my breast,
    O rosy nephew golden-curled;
Boys, birds, and flowers hush to rest,
    So weary grows the world.

As slowly as the branches wave,
    Singing, I rock you to and fro;
So tune be glad, if words are grave
    The baby will not know.

Far off and faint the chirpings sound,
    Pale lights gleam out through dark'ning blue,
Soft arms of silence fold us round.
    As mine are folding you.

Northland Lyrics

Small voice that twitters like the birds,
  Grey eyes that hold the light of stars,
Too sleepy we for tune or words;
  Let down the dreamland bars!

THE GARDEN

A fairy lamb as white as snow
Through all your dreams shall come and go,
And you shall follow where he leads,
Through dusk-deep woods and blossomy meads,
To where a little garden stands
Laid out for you by fairy hands,
Set round with red-coned tamarack, —
Four walls to keep the great world back, —
With lovely avenues, whose shade
From eglantine and spruce is made,
With oread ferns in shady spots,
And shoals of blue forget-me-nots,
With rows of crimson hollyhocks,
And columbine, and spicy stocks,
And other, fairer blossoms known
To folk of childlike heart alone, —
The yellow lily whose romance
Grew not on any field of France,
One white, ethereal immortelle
From those lost woods we loved so well,

Northland Lyrics

And that Blue Rose whose petals gleam
So richly by the paths of dream !

O Baby, let your wee hands keep
Some flowers when you come back from sleep.

THE MEN OF MY HEART'S DESIRE

Where are the men of my heart's desire ?
   Of the British blood and the loyal names ?
Some are North, at the home hearth-fire,
   Where the hemlock glooms and the maple flames,
And some are tramping the old world round
For the pot of gold they have never found.

Oh, leal are the men of my heart's desire —
   Their fathers were leal in the days gone by —
And their blood is blithe with the subtle fire
   The purple breeds, and their hearts are high,—
Poor, and gallant, and dear to me,
With a strong hand each, and a pedigree.

Good men are bred in the East and the West,
   And ripe, true gentles in Boston town,
But the men of my blood to my blood seem best —
   Who still hold the honour of Mitre and Crown.
Though empty their cellars and worn their attire,
These are the men of my heart's desire.

Northland Lyrics

So, Gentles, these stumbling rhymes I send
To our spruce-clad hills, for a word of cheer,—
Where there 's ever a welcome and ever a friend,
And the brown coat covers the cavalier.
Take them, I pray you, for what they are worth,
For I swear by my soul you 're the salt of the earth.

A LAMENT

TO THE MEMORY OF ARCHIBALD LAMPMAN

His was not the glory of the shattering of spears;
He did not cross his sword with Death, where
scarlet flags are hurled,
But Death came to him softly, with his dark eyes
dim with tears,
And broke a dream of woodland-ways across a
singing world.

So doff your hats, good poet-men,
No fingers lift the fallen pen!
The sun forgets to mark the time
Without the music of his rhyme.

His was not the glory of the thundering of wars;
His was not a nation's voice!—are his a nation's
tears?

Northland Lyrics

To him the night-winds whispered all the secrets of
    the stars,
  He was priest of all the joyous springs and of the
    dying years.

    So doff your hats, good gentlemen,
    For hearts were made to bleed again.
    With Archie gone, and all his rhyme,
    Who'll tell the world 't is April-time?

DARGAI RIDGE

Thank God I have in my laggard blood
The vim of the Englishman,
Which is second to none, from North to South,
Save the fire of the Scottish clan —
Save the blood of the lads who died
On the rocky mountain-side,
And went to the hell of the heated guns
As a lover goes to his bride.

The Ghoorkas laughed at the whining balls —
And they were of alien race.
The English drave at the smoking rocks
And their subalterns set the pace.
Oh the blood of the lads who fell
Where the valley lay a hell;

Northland Lyrics

Thank God that the men in the East and West
Cheer at the tale they tell.

The Ghoorkas lay in the slaughter place,
Save a few that had battled through —
Their brown, brave faces raised to the steep
Where the flags of the marksmen flew —
Their great souls cheering still
(Souls that no ball could kill)
Into the ears of the few, who crouched
Under the crooked hill.

The English went as maids to a dance
Or hounds to the huntsman's call,
And the English lay in the valley-lap
And smeared their blood on the wall.
Oh the blood that knows no shame,
And the valour clear of blame —
Thank God that the world is girt about
With the gold of an English name.

Then the men of the Gordon Highlanders
With their bagpipes shrilling free —
The lads of the heather pasture-sides,
The lads of the unclad knee,
Charged — where their friends lay dead —
Over the green and the red

To the cry of the regimental pipes
And the flop of the hitting lead.

They passed the level of sprawling shapes
And the valley of reeking death;
They struck the rocks of the mountain pass
Where the smoke blew up like breath.
Little they thought of fame
Or the lifting of a name;
They only thought of the mountain crest
And the circle of spitting flame.

Thank God I find in my laggard blood,
Deep down, the fire of the man,
And the heart that shakes with a mad delight
At the name of a Highland clan —
At the name of the lads who died
On the rocky mountain-side
And went to the hell of the heated guns
As a lover goes to his bride.

THE BUGLE-CALL.

The night loomed black with coming storm,
  The narrow pass was iron-walled,
And through the dark profound and grim
  A solitary bugle called.

Northland Lyrics

Its voice from cloudy heights unseen
   With sudden summoning sweetness spoke,
And in the heavy heart of time
   Eternity's desire awoke.

Blow loud and clear from height to height,
   O bugle, bid the dark be gone;
Call out across the stormy hills
   The gold and azure wings of dawn!

AT THE END OF A BOOK

When that old Vendor, to whose hand
The loveliest volumes come at last,
Shall thumb you for a trace of good
Enduring though your day be past,

Be not abashed at your small worth;
His sense is keen; and there may cling
About your yellowing pages still
Some freshness of the Northern Spring;

Some echo of the whitethroat's song
From lonely valleys blue with rain,
Ringing across the April dusk
Joy and unfathomable pain;

Some glamor of the darling land
Of purple hill and scarlet tree,
Of tidal rivers and tall ships
And green diked orchards by the sea;

A sweep of elm-treed interval
And gravelly floors where herons wade;
A sigh of wind through old gray barns
With eeriest music ever made.

And will no hint of this outweigh
The faulty aim, the faultier skill,

To save our credit when we come
To the Green Dwelling in the Hill?

Ah, trust the Vendor wise and kind!
He knows the outside and the in,
And loves the very least of those
He tosses in the dusty bin.

BLISS CARMAN.

www.ingramcontent.com/pod-product-compliance
Lightning Source LLC
Chambersburg PA
CBHW031438270326
41930CB00007B/772